"Being the King's name day, I called the town
Guelph, the smaller fry in office having mon-
opolized every other I could think of; and my
friend (the easy-going, hard-drinking, Dr.
'Tiger' Dunlop) drawing a bottle of whiskey
from his bosom, we drank prosperity to the un-
built metropolis of the new world."

* Guelph was the family name of the British
reigning monarch at that time, King George IV.

1   *John Galt, Guelph's founder. The thin smile and almost laughing eyes, delicately captured by the artist's brush, reveal the sometime writer and poet's greatest strength — his flair for the imaginative.*

Frontispiece in John Galt's Autobiography.

TAKE A LOOK
AT US!

THE BOSTON MILLS PRESS

2 *The community centre in 1895 —
St. George's Square. The blacksmith fountain now stands in
Priory Square next to the C.I.A.G.
building.*

The Royal Hotel Collection

4 *A wet, dismal Monday was Guelph's founding day. The date: St. George's Day, April 23,
1827. The actual founding site lies buried
beneath the huge limestone blocks at the west
end of the C.N.R. bridge.*

Guelph: Take A Look At Us
ISBN 0-919822-94-0
Donald E. Coulman

Copyright © The Boston Mills Press

Published in Canada by The Boston Mills Press,
R.R. 1, Cheltenham, Ontario & by Ampersand
Press, Guelph.

The Boston Mills Press gratefully acknowledges the
assistance of the Canada Council and the Ontario
Arts Council in the publishing of this book.

Design by John Denison & Mike McDonald

Printed by Ampersand Press, 14 Eramosa Road,
Guelph, Ontario.

The Boston Mills Press is a small independent Canadian publishing house dedicated to printing local
histories, collectors' handbooks and other special
appeal books. If you are interested in having a book or
pamphlet published, or wish to know more about us,
please feel free to write to the above address. We'll do
all we can to help.

3 Today, a crown adorns St.
George's Square. Look at the interesting comparison provided by
the two photos. The controversial
crown was erected as a Christmas
decoration in 1960.

150 YEARS AGO

Guelph was founded by John Galt, a 48 year old writer, business-man, world traveller and, apparently, sometime smuggler. As General Agent for a large land development enterprise, The Canada Company, he wanted Guelph to be the flagship city in the Huron Tract — a generous slice of heavily forested land between Guelph and Goderich.

The city plan for Guelph was a direct expression of Galt's main concern: people. To him, a community meant more than factories, dwellings, roads and profits. His carefully considered scheme for our city made ample provision for strengthening those things which ensure the survival of a society — the family, a place for worship or reflection, and, education.

It was John Galt's strong commitment to social values that led to his downfall in The Canada Company. The London based company directors disagreed with Galt's use of company profits for local improvements — they wanted a quick return on their investment. These same officials even objected to the name of Guelph; they wanted the city to be called Goderich. (The resulting conflict between Galt and his employers led to the oft told, but inaccurate story that the street plans for Guelph and Goderich got mixed up.)

Guelph has grown in 150 years. It has become "big." Somehow, though, it is still a "small" place where you and I feel that we have a major share in its life — Guelph provides a good sense of self.

Will our city continue to provide that very important feeling: "a good sense of self"? We face many uncertainties; but, the uncertainties are almost the same as those faced by the Guelph pioneers 150 years ago.

Please enjoy the book, you're very much a part of it!

5   With little, except dreams and courage, the Guelph pioneers faced many hardships. This view from College Hill in 1872 shows the yet to be cleared stumps. In the upper centre of the photo, you can see the forerunner of the present Gordon Street bridge.
R.A.M. Stewart

6   The same site two years later. The stumps have been removed in preparation for crop planting. Just beyond the Speed River in the centre of the picture is the present location of the Ponderosa restaurant.   R.A.M. Stewart

7   By 1900, the field was in full crop production. The rugged appearance has disappeared. On the hill in the upper left corner is the Church of Our Lady (without the spires). The field is now a portion of the Cutten Club golf course.

Galt almost didn't accomplish the founding of Guelph on St. George's Day. Prior to his arrival in the yet to be founded city, he and his party had the misfortune of getting lost.

It was an exasperated, but determined man who, along with Dr. "Tiger" Dunlop, Charles Prior and two woodsmen, completed the founding around suppertime on that fourth Monday in April 150 years ago. A large maple tree was cut down to mark Guelph's first day.

Why did John Galt choose this particular site for the City of Guelph? The exact reasons will remain locked forever in John Galt's complex personality. An energetic man of many talents and interests, Galt was a lover of the arts and an imaginative writer. This unusual man also had a strong perception of reality: he was a meticulous organizer and planner; he had a keen sense of "what would work" within his concept of beauty.

To Galt, the site for Guelph had just the "right mixture" of utility and beauty. The Speed River, according to him, had adequate rather than abundant waterpower capabilities. (Later, Galt curiously overestimated the power of the river when he reported to the Governor of Upper Canada that there were 17 potential mill sites at Guelph.) Galt knew that the pleasant, gently-rolling and heavily forested land surrounding Guelph would provide well for the settlers. Although he felt Guelph would not become a major centre for commerce, Galt founded the city almost exactly in the centre of all Upper Canada's major trade routes.

Many different reasons can be found for his decision; but, perhaps, the main reason was simply because John Galt liked it. It suited him.

THE PRIORY

8   "The Priory," built in 1827, was Guelph's first building. John Galt designed it and personally supervised the construction work. (Photograph date: about 1880) Originally, this structure was to be the headquarters for the "Canada Company" — a land holding company which sold lots to individual settlers. Land prices were pretty reasonable in 1827 . . . From an ad in the Ancaster Gore Gazette (October 27, 1827)
    —Town lots, 40 dollars in cash
    —Farm lots of 25, or 50, or 100
    acres, paid in cash, 2 dollars
    per acre. (On credit, $2.50 per acre)
R.A.M. Stewart

9   *Apparently, Guelph's first Civic Banquet was a bit of a disaster since the ox was not cooked enough. Whiskey was in plentiful supply, which probably accounted for the several fights which broke out among the 500 or so guests.*

10   *Stiffly posing for the camera in front of "The Priory" — The Allan family and their gardener (c.1870). David Allan (centre) — son of William Allan, the famous Guelph miller — was an accomplished architect. He designed several Guelph buildings. Among them: the Court House and St. Andrew's Church. "The Priory" was owned by the Allan family from 1838 to 1878.*

Left to Right: Sandy Glass (gardener); William Allan jr.; David Allan; Mrs. Allan; Margaret Jane Allan.
R.A.M. Stewart

11 "The Priory" (c.1900) was a busy place after it became the C.P.R. station in 1887. It remained as a station until the new C.P.R. station (now the Chamber of Commerce building) was built in 1911.

R.A.M. Stewart

12 Elm logs, native to the Guelph area, were used in the construction of the building. John Galt, who made it his home until 1829, was especially proud of the Ionic rustic portico. Numerous tenants came and went throughout "The Priory's" somewhat checkered career. For a time, it housed Guelph's first post office — "The Priory" even served as a temporary refuge for early settlers.

Wally Beadle

"Guelph citizens are up in arms over the high handed persons unknown who swooped into the Royal City and removed its number one historic relic — a portion of the first house built in Guelph in 1827."
(The Daily Mercury, October 5, 1957)

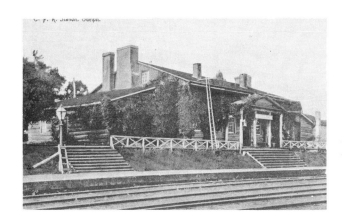

13 "They let it fall to pieces. . ." Ironically, it was torn down in 1926 — one year before Guelph's Centennial. Some of the logs, kept in storage until 1957, were "mysteriously" moved to the Doon Pioneer Village.   The Royal Hotel Collection

14 "The Priory" site in 1976 (arrow). Soon, asphalt for the Wellington Street extension will cover the former location of "The Priory". All that remains of the once proud building is a scale-model replica in Riverside Park.

15   Two boys on Allan's Dam in 1873. The exact date of this photograph is disclosed by the scaffolding surrounding the St. George's Church spire (upper left). The church was built in 1873.   The Royal Hotel Collection

16   A panoramic view of the Allan's Mill area from Galt's Hill (often called Horsman's or Day's Hill) around 1870. Allan's Mill is in the upper right. To the left is a distillery which is now a part of the W.C. Wood Company. Allan's Mill ceased to be a flour mill about 1882. After that, various companies used the building — one was a lightbulb manufacturing business.   R.A.M. Stewart

17   Allan's Mill, 1870.   R.A.M. Stewart

18   In its heyday, Allan's Mill attracted farmers from as far away as Owen Sound. Until recently, all that was left of the massive building was the back portion. Note the remains of an old fireplace (arrow). The Wellington Street extension now covers the former mill site.

THE MILLS

19 "The People's Mills" (Goldie's Mill) in 1894. "Dictator Pastry Flour" and "Snowdrift Bread Flour" were milled from wheat by 6 pairs of stone wheels spun by four, 40 horsepower water turbines. Land development in the Guelph area reduced the volume of water in the river dramatically during the 1880s. Most of the Guelph millers had steam engines installed to provide additional power.

R.A.M. Stewart

20 Most of this impressive stone mill built in 1850 still stands near Norwich and Cardigan streets. Spring floods always worried mill owners. There is a long history of mill pond dams bursting on the Speed River. Goldie's Mill was the last, large flour mill to close its doors (1930).

. . . 1971

21 "Coopers" provided the packaging for flour during the 1800s. The heavy, bulky barrels they made were filled with the milled flour for shipment. James Goldie established a "cooperage", employing 24 men, across the river from his mill. At the peak of the cooperage business, there were 75 coopers in Guelph. The introduction of the sack retired most of them. (Photograph date: c.1885)

R.A.M. Stewart

22 & 23   Look at the remarkable change in the former Speedvale Mill location! The photograph taken around 1870, clearly shows the old Speedvale Avenue bridge. Guelph's second fire hall now occupies the old mill site. By the middle of the 1880s Guelph millers had converted milling stones to the more efficient, and faster, steel rollers. One of the owners of the Speedvale Mill capitalized on this conversion by calling his mill the "Jumbo Mill."   (22) R.A.M. Stewart

24 & 25   The former Victoria Mill in 1964. During the nineteenth century flour milling was one of Guelph's most important businesses; consequently, the mill-owner was usually a most influential and wealthy Guelph citizen.

Fire, a persistent menace to the mills, frequently destroyed all but their solid limestone outershells. The Wellington Street Canadian Tire store parking lot is now located on this site.

Frank Wood

What is home like
  without a Bell organ?
A prison, asylum; a jail
  Where no one will stay
but a culprit
  Unable to find any bail

"*A Panegyric on the*
  Bell Organ" *by George Norrish,*
a Guelph poet and long time
employee of the Bell Organ
Company.

27   Directory, County of Wellington, 1871-2.

26   Bell organs and pianos manufactured in Guelph were shipped to all parts of the world. At the peak of Bell's business (around 1885), the company produced 5000 to 6000 instruments a year and employed 450 people. If you look closely at the lettering on the wall of the Carden Street factory, you can see the company was established in 1864 (by William and Robert Bell) . . . Jubilee Park is in the foreground of the photograph.   Wally Beadle
c.1900

28 Boom times in the organ and piano business encouraged company officials to have this additional manufacturing building constructed in 1881. Notice the large piles of piano and organ cabinet wood in the picture foreground. The Depression, along with aggressive competition from other piano manufacturers, forced the company to close around 1930. c.1895
R.A.M. Stewart

29 Flames leap from an upper window of the old Bell Organ Factory #2, July 16, 1975. Fire gutted this building numerous times throughout its lifetime. For many years, Branch 234 of the Canadian Legion occupied the structure.
Kitchener-Waterloo Record

Silver Creek Brewery. GEO. SLEEMAN, GUELPH, ONT.

"... Endorsed by millions of sensible, thinking men as the most palatable and healthsome of beverages, when judiciously used."

31 The famous "Silver Creek Brewery" business was established by John Sleeman in 1851. His son, well-known George Sleeman, took over in 1861. Compare the number and rows of windows in this brewery advertisement with the actual number in the 1889 photograph of the building.   R.A.M. Stewart

32 The "Silver Creek Brewery" building at the west end of Waterloo Avenue in 1889. Later this structure housed the "Standard Brands" company. The building was removed in 1970 to make way for the Hanlon Expressway. To bottle collectors, a Sleeman's beer bottle is a real treasure.

34 George Sleeman did everything in a big way. His home, "The Manor," located opposite the brewery, is huge. The furnishings were massive: a 22 seat walnut table in the dining room; a large billiard table on the third floor. A favourite with Guelph families was a Sunday afternoon walk to "The Manor" to see the beer-bottle-glass surfaced front sidewalk.

The Royal Hotel Collection

33 George Sleeman rates as one of Guelph's greatest benefactors. This energetic, ambitious citizen served as Mayor on three occasions and was involved in innumerable civic and business activities. Sleeman even had a street railway built for the city in 1895!

Atlas of Wellington County, 1906

35 Sleeman business envelope.

Wally Beadle

36 Sons William and Tindale inherited the brewery. . . Apparently, they were as sterling as their father, being "substantial business men, active in the promotion of every interest looking to the good and welfare of the city, and liberal contributors to every movement having as its object her advancement along any legitimate line." ("Souvenir Industrial Number of the Evening Mercury of Guelph" — 1908)   R.A.M. Stewart

37 "He always took more pride in the making of good ale than in the accumulation of wealth. He was an able man, energetic, skilful and magnetic; of fine physique , with many friends, and a knowledge of the world obtained by travel. He detested dishonesty and never drew a line between meanness and dishonesty, and his word was considered as good as his bond; an Englishman of the old school, he was dignified, and of rather austere manner, but underneath this awkward mask of austerity, there beat one of the kindest hearts in the world. . ."

The 1906 Wellington County Atlas

38 "East Kent Ale" was brewed at the Holliday Brewery. The business was established in the mid-1800s by Thomas Holliday. In this photograph, taken around 1900, you can clearly see the brewery and the brewmaster's house to the far left.

Mrs. V.W. Burrows

39 The remains of the brewery still stand at the corner of Yorkshire and Bristol streets. In the nineteenth century, there were no less than four distilleries and two breweries in Guelph.

41 Stern looking company founder, Robert Stewart. A carpenter and joiner by trade, Mr. Stewart was president of the business for 64 years. Many described him as a man with a "rugged constitution." His grandson, Robert A. Stewart, has, over the years, collected a great many Guelph historical pictures, documents and furniture. Robert Stewart jr.'s office desk once belonged to mill owner, James Goldie. R.A.M. Stewart

40 S.I. Turner

Stewarts Planing Mill and Lumber Yard.

42 The Great Fire of Guelph, Wednesday, July 6, 1921. It began with a blinding flash of flame at 4:00 in the morning. Within 15 minutes it was a seething inferno which reduced the Stewart Lumber Company and several other upper Wyndham Street buildings to ashes. Across the road, Wellington Hotel guests were being prepared for immediate evacuation. The spectacular fire resulted in more than 1 million dollars damage. The Guelph post office now stands on the former Stewart Lumber building site. R.A.M. Stewart

43 Hat covered employees in front of the Wyndham Street Robert Stewart Lumber Company building (c.1875). Established by Robert Stewart in 1854, the company is reputed to be one of the oldest businesses in Canada. A company centennial advertisement in 1954 claimed: "75% of Guelph is built with Stewart lumber."

R.A.M. Stewart

RAYMOND
SEWING MACHINE FACTORIES

GUELPH. - ONTARIO.

45 The sewing machine mogul's business flourished. Raymond bought out the Arms & Worswick Sewing Machine Company building at the corner of Suffolk and Yarmouth streets. Fire destroyed the building in 1875 and Raymond replaced it with the stone structure seen in this photograph taken about 1895. (Notice the steeple of St. Andrew's Church at the far right.)

The Royal Hotel Collection

44 After suffering through legal battles over sewing machine patents in the United States, American born Charles Raymond arrived in Guelph in 1862 to set up a major Guelph manufacturing enterprise. Many of Raymond's substantial sewing machines still exist today. Interestingly, most of the machines were shipped to Germany. The photograph, taken around 1874, shows the factory on Yarmouth Street (Norfolk Street in the foreground). The Raymond home is on the left.

R.A.M. Stewart

"A Firm that has been identified with all
the ups and downs of Guelph for the last
forty-five years, and one that has done its
share towards promoting the general welfare of the city is The Raymond Manufacturing Company."

...from a 1906 Guelph advertising
booklet... Elizabeth Gray.

46 A roaring fire destroyed the old frame factory in 1875. Almost immediately, construction was started on a new brick building (right) which still stands today. (Cooke and Denison building — you can still read the large "Raymond's Sewing Machine" lettering across the top of the building.) After the fire, a number of Raymond employees helped form the "Guelph Victoria Volunteer Fire Company."

The former Raymond home was torn down to make way for a larger, ornate Italian Victorian house called "Lornewood." The park in the foreground is where the public library now stands.

R.A.M. Stewart

47 Suffolk and Yarmouth streets in 1976. At the height of the business, the Raymond factory complex was, indeed, sprawling. Besides buildings on Yarmouth Street and Suffolk Street, there was a large building on Baker Street (now the Baker Street parking lot). Charles Raymond sold out in 1896. The firm operated until 1916, when the new owner, The White Sewing Machine Company, moved the business and equipment to Cleveland, Ohio.

48   The Burrows Brothers' employees about 1892.
(Notice the bowler hats.) Did they like their work?
No one's smiling. You would wonder whether the
two youngsters at either end of the photograph were
permanent employees. Notice the three ladies in the
side doorway. The building was located on the now
very controversial lot on the south-west corner of
Norfolk and Paisley streets.   Mrs. V.W. Burrows

THE MARKETS

GUELPH WOOD YARD.

THE undersigned is now prepared to deliver to any part of the town good Beech and Maple Cordwood at $4 per cord, or $2 for a half cord.— Also for sale a quantity of good, sound Rock Elm at $3 per cord. He will constantly keep on hand good Cedar for kindling wood, at $3 per cord, or $1.50 for half a cord. I guarantee that a full cord in each case will be delivered.

☞ Orders left at No. 4 Butcher's Stall, Market House, or at the Yard opposite Deady's Hotel, will be promptly attended to. Terms strictly cash.

JOHN WEST.

TO THE PUBLIC.

THE Undersigned having bought out No. 4 Stall, lately occupied by Mr. R. Cochrane, is prepared to sell meat of the very best quality at the lowest possible prices for cash.

JOHN WEST.

Guelph, 13th June, 1867.

49

By-Law No. 146 (1887) "A By-Law to Regulate the Manner of Selling and Measuring Firewood."
"Firewood offered for sale, or sold by the cord, or aliquot* part of a cord shall be fairly, closely and compactly piled by the vendor thereof, and no such firewood shall be deceitfully or unfairly piled, so as to appear to be of greater measure than if it were fairly, closely and compactly piled; and no crooked wood shall be piled with such firewood, but the same shall be packed or piled separately, and in any measurement thereof, under this by-law, due allowance shall be made for such crooked wood.
*aliquot: exact division of a whole part.
. . . The chief constable and police officers were firewood inspectors — fee: 10¢/cord.

50 The "Guelph Woodmarket" in 1874. Kindling Wood for warmth and cooking was a major nineteenth century market item. Just visible to the right is the city hall.
The Royal Hotel Collection

51 Carden Street about 1870. The old vegetable market is to the left. The city hall is just behind the market building. The carriage (right) is a nineteenth century style taxi used to take train passengers uptown to the various hotels.

R.A.M. Stewart

52 Carden Street as it appears today. The vegetable market was torn down in 1887 when Jubilee Park was created. The land was expropriated in 1911 for the construction of the C.N.R. station. Notice the two very old buildings at the end of Carden Street. They've been there a long time!

1887 Bylaw . . . For Regulating the Market
Section 16.
No person shall go to any place in the city of Guelph to meet anyone bringing into the city Guelph market for sale grains, woods, meats, fruits, roots, vegetables, poultry, butter, eggs, dairy produce, or any other article or articles required for family use, and such as are usually sold in the market, for the purpose of buying, or proposing to buy or bargain, for any such article by the way, and before the same is brought to the market.

53 The marketplace about 1885. The building in the centre contained the market clerk's office and the weigh scales. Just to the right of this building you can see hay wagons loaded with hay for market. The sign on the wagon in the right foreground says "Massey Harris."

The Royal Hotel Collection

54 Guelph City Hall c.1867. Mayor John Smith presided over the cornerstone laying ceremony, Thursday, September 18, 1856. The cornerstone contains newspapers, statistical documents, an 1855 Guelph map, and several Victoria coins as well as one Canada penny. After the usual speeches and the playing of God Save the Queen, there was a big party at Horwood's Hotel. The Royal Hotel Collection

"Guelph does nothing by halves; neither does she go blindly into anything that has not been tried. Conservative thought, keen insight, sound judgement and careful investigation have characterized every progressive step in every crisis."

... from a 1906 Guelph Ad.

NOTICE

A GREAT PUBLIC MEETING SHALL TAKE PLACE AT THE MARKET PLACE

On August 6th, 1827, A.D., for the express and proclaimed purposes of acquainting one to the other of our people, and further that they may free themselves of the different thoughts, suggestions, and imaginations pertaining to the welfare of our town, and to devise ways and means of inducing businesses of manufacture to venture the establishment of their properties in this village.

It is proposed that an association should be formed and known as the Board of Commerce.

(NO WRANGLING ALLOWED) August 1st, 1827.

The Guelph Winter Fair building (now part of Memorial Gardens) was officially opened December 7, 1909. Largely due to the efforts of the widely-known Guelph Fat Stock Club, the Ontario Government decided, in 1900, that Guelph should be the centre for the annual Provincial Winter Fair. The Guelph event was doomed when the Toronto Royal Winter Fair was established in 1921.

Guelph's first fair in May, 1828, had five entries: 3 cows and 2 yoke of oxen. It seems that a good brawl was an accepted part of the city's earliest agricultural shows. The first show was no exception — for no apparent reason, a fight broke out at the "Horn of Plenty" tavern. Combatants: "Irishmen" vs "Yankees". As the word of the melee spread, it wasn't long before everyone in every Guelph tavern was fighting. It isn't recorded which side won.

City Hall and Winter Fair Building, Guelph, Ont

55 The city hall's famous designer, William Thomas, would have been shocked if he had seen the tall dome the 1869 City Council authorized to be placed on the building. The tower was unceremoniously removed in 1961. (Among architect Thomas' designs was Toronto's well known St. Lawrence Hall.) Guelph became a town in 1856 and a full-fledged city in 1879. Postcard photograph date: c.1900. Wally Beadle

GUELPH, ONTARIO—THE ROYAL CITY
A CITY OF GREAT ENTERPRISES—WHOLESALE AND MANUFACTURING
· · · · · · · AGRICULTURAL RESOURCES UNSURPASSED · · · · · ·

57 **Guelph Fat Stock Club** members in front of City Hall about 1910. The group arranged highly popular cattle shows in Guelph. Many of the club members were also city aldermen or officials. Notice the two men looking on from behind the two windows.

Frances Peer

58   The magnificent illuminated arch in St. George's Square.

59   Guelph's 100th birthday being celebrated in front of the City Hall on a cold April 23, 1927. One member of the choir remembers: "We stood up there freezing to death!" Mayor Bev Robson (centre) is wearing the silk hat.

Aileen Cooke

60   Centennial festivities chairman, Alderman Harry Mahoney.

62   One of the Centennial attractions: "The Guelph Jazz Band" in St. George's Square. Almost everyone remembers the week long celebration enthusiastically: "We had a wonderful time — there was dancing in the streets — The big part was to get dressed up in a costume so that you wouldn't be known — then you could do what you wanted."

Chris V. Robinson

63   Centennial Hi-jinx in St. George's Square. "The celebration was a wild party! There was no shortage of fun!" exclaimed one Guelphite who was in on the festivities.

Wally Beadle

All the photographs on this page courtesy of Dr. R.L. Mahoney.

GUELPH CENTENNIAL

1827 ~ 1927

61 The Royal Dairy Float.

64 Guelph's 1879 Central Exhibition was opened by the Marquis of Lorne and Queen Victoria's daughter, Princess Louise. This huge welcoming arch was erected across lower Wyndham Street. (Many old photographs were made especially for stereoscopic viewers — This is one of them. Notice that a portion of the left photograph remains in this copy of an original stereoscopic view.)   R.A.M Stewart

65 Jubilee Park was "black with humanity" to greet the Duke and Duchess of Cornwall and York (later King George V and Queen Mary), October 12, 1901. Look carefully for the two brave fellows on top of the hydro pole in the upper left corner of the photograph.
R.A.M. Stewart

66 On the eve of the Second World War, King George VI and Queen Elizabeth visited Guelph. Just behind the Royal Couple is Mayor William Taylor. The welcoming stand is just in front of the former Legion building on Carden Street.   Wally Beadle

67 Guelphites were only provided a fleeting glimpse of Queen Elizabeth II and Prince Philip, June 28, 1973. The shiny Royal train slowed down to 3 m.p.h. as it passed through Guelph.

The Daily Mercury

Royal Visits

68 Galt's Hill (known to many as Horsman's Hill or Day's Hill) in 1870. In the foreground is Woolwich Street and the site where St. George's Church is now built. The footbridge has yet to be constructed. "Ker Cavan," Archdeacon Palmer's home, is on the hill (centre). "Prospect Place," (far right) was the spacious home Guelph contractor, John Thorp, built for himself in 1855.

Dorothy and Jack Watkins

69 The old footbridge around 1900. This bridge was replaced with the present bridge in 1913. St. George's Church is at the far left. Huddled under the wrinkled black drape — one hand squeezing the red shutter bulb — the other tightly clutching a tall holder for the blinding flash producing powder, the old time photographer treated onlookers to a real thrill. The spectators on the bridge appear to be enjoying every minute of it!

Dorothy and Jack Watkins

ST. GEORGE'S CHURCH GUELPH.

70 St. George's Church at the turn of the century. This impressive church was opened April 20, 1873. The original church stood in St. George's Square (1833 to 1873). Wally Beadle

71 Archdeacon Palmer, the first rector of St. George's Church, served from 1832 to 1875. He is reported to have said that he emigrated to Canada because it "was a sort of Eldorado for young men with more brains than money."

R.A.M. Stewart

72 Palmer's lavish home, "Kyr Cathleen," (later called "Ker Cavan") on Stuart Street, was built in 1856. The architect was reputed to be Sir Charles Barry, who also designed the British Houses of Parliament. This photograph, taken in about 1870 shows the rear of the house. Palmer's daughter is sitting side saddle on the horse. R.A.M. Stewart

73 St. Bartholomew's Church at the head of Macdonell Street in 1877. The carriage (right) is in front of the Albion Hotel. John Galt personally had the Canada Company grant this commanding site (known earlier as "Church Hill") to Bishop Alexander Macdonell.* Galt did this in thanks for Macdonell's counsel on Upper Canada affairs in the formation days of the Canada Company.

There is an intense controversy surrounding the spelling and pronunciation of the word "Macdonell." Many claim it should be spelled with two "n's". Macdonell's signature, reproduced in the book "Reminiscences of the Late Hon. and Right Rev. Alexander Macdonell," reveals a one "n" Macdonell.

The second part of the controversy is not so easily solved. One local history book strongly suggests that "Macdonell" should be pronounced Mac-don-ell with emphasis on the first and last syllable. Apparently, pronouncing the word like "MacDonald" is just not correct.

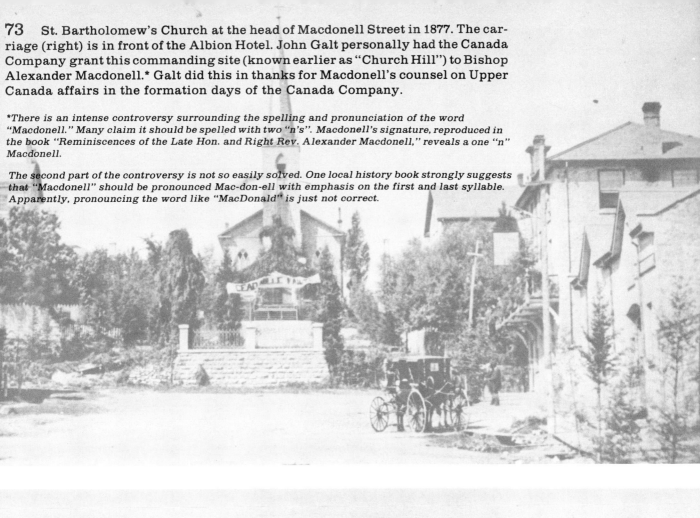

74 The Church of Our Lady, 1890. The first sod for this magnificent church was turned in 1876 — the cornerstone was laid in 1877. A rather unconventional way was used to build the church. Workmen completed the back part of the new church up to the rear wall of the old St. Bartholomew's. The wall was torn down and construction proceeded to slowly engulf the old church. St. Bartholomew's was completely demolished in 1887. The tall Church of Our Lady spires were built in 1926.

75 A view up Norfolk Street in 1870. In the "old days" many of Guelph's sidewalks were "board-walks." St. Andrew's Church (constructed in 1857) with its 150 foot tall spire can be seen in the background. To the right is the first Raymond home. The city bought the original St. Andrew's Church and property to build the city hall.

The Royal Hotel Collection

76 Knox Presbyterian Church around 1905. The Knox congregation was established in 1844 by a group of St. Andrew's members who favoured a "free" Presbyterian church not associated with a political state. This church was built in 1868.

Dorothy and Jack Watkins

77 Dissenters from Knox formed the Chalmer's Church Congregation. It was a hot June day (notice the sun-shielding umbrellas) in 1870 when the cornerstone for Chalmer's Church was laid. The back of St. George's Church in the square is on the right. On the far left is the original Wellington Hotel.

R.A.M. Stewart

Dublin Street and Methodist Church, Guelph, Ont., Canada

78 Dr. Egerton Ryerson, a staunch Methodist preacher and champion Ontario educator, officially opened Dublin Street United Church in January, 1876.

Wally Beadle

79 With well groomed mutton-chops, Rev. S. Sellery of the Second Wesleyan Methodist Church (now Dublin Street United Church), provided a relaxed portrait for the camera in 1890. Do the gently compassionate eyes reveal anything about this man's character?

Dr. R.L. Mahoney

EDUCATION

"Education is a subject so important to a community that it obtained my earliest attention, and accordingly in planning the town I stipulated that half of the price of the building sites should be appropriated to endow a school..." John Galt

80   The pupils of North-ward School around 1870. Later, well known St. George's School was con-structed on the site. Galt's Academy (more popularly known as the "Stone School") was the first school built in Guelph in the late 1820s. Located just behind the west end of the C.N.R. bridge, this one room stone structure was abandoned in 1854.   R.A.M. Stewart

There were no school taxes in the early days of Guelph. Each pupil paid 25¢ per month or its equi-valent in "flour, pork, wood or other trade." One teacher was nicknamed "Cash" Carroll: he accep-ted cash only, no credit.

81 Going to school around 1922. In the early 1800s school attendance was voluntary. One 1843 Guelph area school official complained: "It is not fair that the children of the idle, the reprobate, and the careless should run wild in the streets and highways, learning little but evil themselves, and corrupting others."

82 Central School, 1889. A vast number of Guelphites have passed through the doors of this fine limestone building which was opened Tuesday, January 16, 1877. The new Central School was built in 1969.

It has a reputation
That's built up through the years,
So let us give old Central,
A round of three good cheers.
...Ted Chase, former Central student.

83 The Ontario Agricultural College about 1905. In the background is the original administration building, Johnston Hall. Although this structure is gone, the portico still remains on campus. Notice the cannon which i by tradition, often garishly painted (usually in the dead of night) by prank-loving undergraduate students.　　　Wally Beadle

SCHOOLS

84   The students and teachers of The Guelph Collegiate Institute around 1890. Until the construction of John F. Ross Collegiate Vocational Institute in 1956, virtually everyone in Guelph went to G.C.V.I.
R.A.M. Stewart

The O.A.C. started humbly in 1873 when the Ontario Government paid F.W. Stone $75,000 for his 500 acre "Moreton Lodge Farm." 30 students enrolled on May 1, 1874 for the first class. They worked seven hours a day in the barns and fields. Lodging and board were free — $50 was given to each "aggie" who passed his examinations. The University of Guelph has grown to become Guelph's biggest culutural and economic benefactor.

85   A car on the steps of Mac-Donald Hall . . . O.A.C. pranksters always seem to achieve the impossible!
Wally Beadle

THE LAW

86 An almost overbearing yet, somehow, gently regal court house (c.1910). David Allan designed this building completed in 1843. Notice the horse hitches on the little front lawn.

Some court cases reported in the Saturday Morning Sun, October 15, 1887. . .

"Nancy Dolan went to the refinery for six months. Vagrancy.
"James Wilson, of Brampton, got paralyzed and the Sergt. ran him in. $1 and costs was the damages."

The Public Archives of Canada

87 Police Chief Frederick W. Randall maintained "excellent order" in Guelph for 38 years. When he arrived from Toronto in 1881, "Guelph was full of crime and disorderly places." Randall, a crack pistol shot, won innumerable revolver competition trophies. Described by many as very stern yet fair, he was so dedicated that he stopped by the police station every night "just to check on things." When he retired in 1919, his "pension" was to become the Chief of Puslinch — a less than onerous job in those days.

Frances Peer

88 The Guelph Police Force on the city hall steps in 1928.

FRONT ROW: (L. to R.) A.E. Lamb (later Chief), Bob Brash, Constable McCord, Chief Alex Rae, Angus McGregor, John ("Taillight") Teevens.[1]

BACK ROW: (L. to R.) James Whitelaw, Crown Attorney J.M. Kearns, Mayor R. Beverley Robson, Magistrate Frederick Watt, Detective Phil Hauck, Don Smith.

[1] So the story goes, "Taillight" Teevens, a very popular policeman, picked up his nickname one evening when he stopped a Guelph motorist whose car taillights were off. Teevens reprimanded the driver and proceeded to write out a ticket. The quick minded motorist noted that there was a power failure and the street lights were out. He said, pointing to the lifeless street lamps: "Sure the taillights are out. How can you expect them to be on when the power's off!" With that "Taillight" let him go and the nickname stuck.

Unlike now, getting to the scene of an accident or crime a few years ago took a Guelph policeman some time — no matter how furiously he pedalled his bike!

Robert W. Warden, Guelph Police Department

89 The volunteers of the Guelph Fire Brigade stand beside their steam fire engine in 1878. They organized on Monday, practiced on Tuesday and went to their first real fire on Wednesday.   Ted Ernst, Guelph Fire Department.

90 The men and equipment of the Guelph Fire Department in front of the old Wilson Street fire station around 1910. The time honoured "bucket brigade" served Guelph in the early days. This hand to hand system was usually very ineffective. After a furious blaze, about the only thing left of a building would be the limestone shell; the wood interior was normally reduced to ashes.
Ted Ernst, Guelph Fire Department

FIRE!

91 A single stream of water extinguishes the last burning embers of the 1921 Robert Stewart Company fire on upper Wyndham Street. A permanent Guelph fire fighting force was started in 1909. There was a Chief, 2 drivers, 4 firefighters and 10 volunteers.   Dr. R.L. Mahoney

92 A 1927 Centennial photograph of a completely mechanized Guelph Fire Department. Gone forever were the bucket brigades, hand operated pumper, steam fire engine, horses and easily broken leather hoses. The department's first motorized vehicle, bought in 1917, was the "Little Red Devil," a car for the Chief.

Ted Ernst, Guelph Fire Department

93 The Fire Department's horsedrawn hose wagon on upper Wyndham Street during Guelph's First World War Peace Day Parade, July 18, 1919. In the beginning years, the volunteer firefighters would commandeer a local cabman's horses to pull the fire engine to a blaze. Upon hearing the fire alarm ringing out during slack business times, cabmen and their teams would race each other to the storage place of Guelph's only fire pumper.   The Royal Hotel Collection

94 The Grand Trunk Railway station about 1895. The first train to arrive in Guelph, January 30, 1856, was greeted by a large cheering crowd. The Grand Trunk Railway later became part of the Canadian National Railway system. (Notice the city hall with its ungainly tower in the background.) Look carefully at the well dressed fellow (centre) who is seemingly strutting for the two ladies heading towards him. In 1885, more than ten passenger trains passed daily through Guelph.

The Royal Hotel Collection

Ontario Provincial Winter Fair
Guelph, December 9th to 12th, 1913

RAILWAY CERTIFICATE

This is to Certify that *A R Wood*
of ....is an Exhibitor or Judge at the above Exhibition for 1913, and as such is entitled to tickets for his personal use from...to Guelph and return, at **one first-class fare,** with minimum charge of 25 cents, at any time between Dec. 5th, 1913, and Dec. 12th, 1913, inclusive, as per arrangement with the various Railway Companies.

.................*R. W. Wade*.......Secretary

This Certificate must be presented to the Railway Ticket Agent each time a Ticket is required. He will detach one coupon each time a Ticket is issued and take up this Certificate the last time. Not more than one Ticket can be purchased each day.

No. **616**

95 Wally Beadle

96 A typical Grand Trunk Railway engine (1873). The C.I.A.G. building is now located on the site just behind this old engine.

97 The Guelph C.P.R. station about 1915. Notice the hardwheeled truck parked beside the building. The last C.P.R. passenger train pulled into this station November 19, 1960. Built in 1911, the building is now occupied by the Guelph Chamber of Commerce.

Wally Beadle

DID YOU KNOW that Guelph owns a railroad? The city owned "Guelph Junction Railway" tracks extend from Goldie's Mill to Guelph Junction (16 miles). The line, opened in 1888, is leased to the C.P.R. for 99 years. Guelph gets a lucrative 40% of all the receipts. The G.J.R. directors even struck a bargain with the C.P.R. that there would be no C.P.R. train diversions around Guelph. In 1921, the competing Grand Trunk Railway (now C.N.) complained loudly about the aggressive advertising tactics of the Guelph Junction Railway. Wally Beadle

98 The magnificent 6167 in action!

When the engine was retired, it was purchased by the city's own Guelph Junction Railway as a 1967 Canada Centennial project.

99   A broken rail caused this serious train accident at Trainor's Cut, near the intersection of #7 highway and Watson Road, on a cold February day in 1907. Four persons were killed and 65 passengers were injured when four cars toppled down the embankment. When this photograph was taken, a temporary track was being built to get the cars back on the mainline.

H.W. Kellington

100   The ominous creaking sounds of the old Guelph Junction Railway (C.P.R.) trestle north of Eramosa Road gave the crew of the train lots of warning to get clear. (August 30, 1895) The heavy 90 ton engine, which was shunting rail cars belonging to Sell's Brothers Circus, could not be moved to safety quickly enough as the woodwork of the trestle slowly broke up.

R.A.M. Stewart

101 This spectacular accident occurred at Gourock (a few miles southwest of Guelph) in 1906. A mixed train unit hit a fruit train special head-on killing two engineers and one fireman. Old timers in the area can vividly remember oranges from the fruit train being strewn everywhere. Even today, local farmers plowing their crop fields occasionally dig up remnants of this wreck.

R.A.M. Stewart

102 Just a few miles from the Gourock disaster, this C.N. engine tore up 140 feet of track after being derailed by a dump truck at the Fife Road crossing in October, 1974. Fortunately, no one was badly injured.

Few words for our Town Innkeepers,
        I hope you won't get tight,
Carry out your business decently from
                morning until night,
So as our visitors by the thousands
            will return and have to say
They've been treated in our town of
    Guelph in a kind and friendly way.

Guelph Poet, James Gay — 1875.

103   A Guelph hotel barroom about 1895.   The Royal Hotel Collection

104   The Jones American Hotel was built in the mid-nineteenth century. For a time in the early 1870s this building housed Central School classes while a new school was being built on Dublin Street. For years, this building which was removed in 1964, belonged to the Guelph Cartage Company.

Today, the Jones American Hotel site is the Stoddart Motors used car lot (formerly B&R Motors). In 1888, there were 22 hotels in Guelph. (Photograph date: c.1865)

H O T E L S

105 The Wellington Hotel, 1889.

106 Massie's Saltyard, 1874. Construction for the Wellington Hotel was started on this site in 1876. In the background is St. George's Church.

R.A.M. Stewart

"The Wellington Hotel, one of the leading houses in Guelph, is an attractive four-storey stone building, admirably heated, lighted and ventilated, and equipped with ample accomodations for the travelling public and especially commercial men for whom spacious sample rooms are furnished.

An ad in the 1908 "Souvenir Industrial Number of the Evening Mercury of Guelph."

107 An electrical short resulted in a horrifying fire which gutted the Wellington Hotel in the early hours of July 7, 1975. Tragically, two hotel guests lost their lives.

Entrance to Riverside Park.   GUELPH, Canada.

108   The entrance to Riverside Park around 1910. "It was a way out of town in those days!" The two little signs at either side of the larged curved sign say: "No Driving Allowed." The park was also a favourite summer camping spot.

The Royal Hotel Collection

109   Riverside Park Superintendent Nicols and his wife in 1932.   Dr. R.L. Mahoney

110   "Half the time we never had a bathing suit. We mostly skinny-dipped or wore our underwear. One trick was to tie our jersey between our legs... The girls weren't around — they never acted like boys then."   Wally Beadle

RIVERSIDE PARK, GUELPH

111 A couple of Guelph bathing beauties around 1925.

Margaret Purdy

112 "Roughing it" about 1910 on the present Reformatory grounds. There were no government operated campgrounds in those days!

Dr. R.L. Mahoney

From the By-laws of the City of Guelph, 1887....

BATHING IN PUBLIC WATERS

37.   No person shall bathe or swim or wash his or her person in any public water within the municipality, at any time during the day or night; provided, however, that any persons wearing a proper bathing dress or costume sufficient to prevent indecent exposure of the person, may bathe in such waters at any time and at any place not nearer than one hundred feet from any public bridge crossing a stream within the municipality; and provided while bathing such persons to not approach nearer than the said distance from any such bridge, and also provided that such bathing dress be put on and taken off without any indecent public exposure of the person.

38. And it is hereby declared that any dress shall be considered hereunder a proper bathing dress, which completely covers or conceals from view that part of the body extending from the waist to two inches above the knee.

113 Lawn Bowling on the front lawn of James Steele's home, 1908.

114 A reserved looking championship baseball team — the 1874 "Guelph Maple Leafs." George Sleeman (centre), a fanatic baseball supporter, took his team to Watertown, N.Y. The club brought home the United States and Canada championship along with $500. While in the States, Pitcher Billy Smith won first prize for the longest baseball throw. No one knows how far he threw the ball but everyone agreed that "it was remarkably long." On the way home, the Leafs played a courtesy game with a Cobourg team — Score: 40 to 3 for the Leafs.

GUELPH MAPLE LEAFS, WORLD AMATEUR CHAMPIONS IN 1874

This achievement at Watertown, N.Y., followed three successive years as Canadian champions. The players as depicted, reading from left to right, were, top row: Bob Emory, rf; William Sunley, p; Billy Jones, 2b; George Kerrel, ss. Middle row: H. Myers, 1b; George Sleeman, president and manager; Billy Smith, cf and p; Harry Spence, 3b. Below: Charlie Maddock, c.

115 The "Guelph Nationals" hockey team around 1900. The "Nationals" reached the O.H.A. finals in 1899 — One player, "Cooney" Shields, had the unnerving habit of removing his glass eye while playing a game. One had to be durable to play hockey then — the 7 man team played two, 30 minute periods without substitutes. Suspecting "professionalism", the O.H.A. suspended the Guelph Nationals from the league in 1900.

TOP ROW (Left to Right):
  W. "Cooney" Shields; Billy Barber; W.A. Raymo; R. Morrison.
BOTTOM ROW:
  Dr. Stirton; "Hoosey" Snell; Dr. H.O. "Rooster" Howitt; Jack Carmichael; E.M. Stewart.

R.A.M. Stewart

116 As it was in the Twenties, tennis is still a summer favourite with many Guelph people.

Dr. R.L. Mahoney

117 Skating on the Speed River near Edinburgh Road, 1870. During the summer, Guelphites of yesteryear apparently turned to roller skates — reported The Guelph Mercury: "Harry Peer skated 186 miles in ten hours at Victoria Roller Rink" (August 27, 1908).

R.A.M. Stewart

TRANSPORTATION

118   A metal bending smash-up at the corner of the Eden Mills road and #7 Highway, July 9, 1938.

119 A Silver Creek Brewery wagon delivering beer to the Western Hotel (now the Ambassador) on Macdonell Street around 1900. Just outside town in the early 1800s, you had to pay a toll to travel the then privately owned Gordon Street. Tolls: (one way) single horse, 5¢; team, 10¢. These roads were bought up by the government after 1859.
R.A.M. Stewart

120 When the horse was "king of the road" in Guelph, there were numerous blacksmith shops throughout the city. This is Sallow's establishment on the northwest corner of Gordon and Wellington streets around 1870.
R.A.M. Stewart

121 Muller's on Woolwich Street had been in business for six years when this 1914 photograph was taken. According to an 1898 report, "Guelph's "Strongman" Teddy Armstrong, was "as strong as a horse." In a show of strength outside city hall, Teddy was able to hold back two horses tethered to each of his outstretched arms.
R.A.M. Stewart

122 Mrs. George Sleeman is driving the first spike for Guelph's street railway system on May 1, 1895. The ceremony is taking place in front of her husband's Silver Creek Brewery. George Sleeman financed the whole street car system with his own money.

R.A.M. Stewart

123 Car #219 was making its first run early in the morning of August 11, 1936. Suddenly, a fast moving car slammed into the front of the streetcar. The three occupants of the auto, who were returning from a baseball game in Owen Sound, were badly cut.

124 An old street car grinds to a halt, at the intersection of Woolwich Street (Elora Road) and London Road about 1912. The marker on the car reads "Riverside Park". The city took over the operation of the Guelph Radial Railway in 1903. The last streetcar rumbled down the rails in 1938.

Wally Beadle

125 All aboard for Toronto! A Toronto Suburban Railway electric train awaits passengers in front of the C.N.R. station about 1920. Proclaimed one former passenger: "The thing went so fast, swayed so much that I thought it would leave the tracks at every one of the umpteen million sharp curves on the line." The T.S.R. line was in operation from 1917 to 1931.... It was a victim of the car, Depression and the competing C.N. railway mainline which it paralleled for many miles.   Gib Kingsbury

Toronto Suburban Railway Co.

No. 11.3338   Form 6

Jan	Feb	Frm	TO	
Mar	A.	★	WEST TORONTO	
May	Jun	★	LAMBTON JUNCTION	
July	Aug	★	ISLINGTON	
Sept	Oct	★	EATON FARM	
Nov	Dec	★	SUMMERVILLE	
1	2	★	DIXIE	
3	4	★	COOKSVILLE	
5	6	★	CENTRE ROAD	NO STOP-OVER ALLOWED
7	8	★	STREETSVILLE	
9	10	★	MEADOWVALE	
11	12	★	CHURCHVILLE	
13	14	★	HUTTONVILLE	
15	16	★	NORVAL	
17	18	★	GEORGETOWN	
19	20		LIMEHOUSE	PASSENGER'S COUPON
21	22	★	DOLLY VARDEN	
23	24	★	ACTON	
25	26	★	BLUE SPRINGS	
27	28	★	EDEN MILLS	
29	30	★	ERAMOSA	
31		★	GUELPH	

EXPRESS		85	90	95	$1
‡		65	70	75	80
		45	50	55	60
HALF FARE		25	30	35	40
‡	3	5	10	15	20

126

127 A panoramic view of Carden Street east from the city hall tower in 1927. The C.N. station is to the right. A combination express and passenger Toronto Suburban Railway radial car can be seen in front of the station. The T.S.R. maintained a 2 hour schedule to Toronto. Many Guelphites considered the T.S.R. to be "kind of a novelty, a street car in the country." Although the tracks are gone, the former rail bed, beginning at the east end of James Street, is clearly visible for many miles. It makes a pleasant Sunday afternoon walk.

The Guelph Daily Mercury, Centennial Issue, July 20, 1927 — Courtesy of Marie Ridd.

128 The switch in motive power is now complete. Now the horses do the riding! Ready to leave for the races, "King" Hillis' three harness horses peer from the back of Mr. Humphrey's "Beaver" truck. "King" is holding the rope firmly tied to the goat standing on the truck's engine hood. The picture was snapped in St. George's Square about 1921.

R.A.M. Stewart

129 Horace Mack stands proudly (about 1922) beside the Gilson care he helped build. All told, three of these cars were built in Guelph: one wasn't finished, one burned in a garage and the third was driven by Gilson executive, Mack.

R.A.M. Stewart

130 A sedate looking "Reo" in 1927. Guelph's Robson Motor Company was having a special sale of the "New and Finer Pontiac Six Coupe" in August, 1927 — Price tag: $930.00. Mr. George Williams, a local baker, received Licence #121 in 1903 for his four passenger Cadillac Runabout. It was the first motor vehicle licence issued in Guelph.

Dr. R.L. Mahoney

131 The dapper men of the Swift's advertising department in 1935. Window dressing in the Guelph area was their specialty.

Aileen Cooke

Getting to Guelph from Toronto in a car was easy in 1912. All you had to do was follow the instructions! . . .

"Leaving Toronto at mile 0.0, drive 46.5 miles to Acton, turn right at hotel, left at 47.8, right at 48.7, left at 49, right at 49.8, left at 51.7, at 53.6 winding road over railway; at 54, turn right, at 54.6 left, at top of hill.

"At mile 55.3 is Rockwood, turn to left, follow telegraph poles, railway to right; pass church at 58.1; down straight hill; at 61.7, follow poles, jog to right at 62.3, to Guelph Station; then turn sharp to 63.0 Guelph."

"Official Automobile Guide of Canada," 1912

132 The Royal City Garage in 1925. This garage on Woolwich Street, featured "Red Indian Motor Oils" and "Marathon Gasoline." Driving up the ramp of the outdoor grease pit probably took some skill! In the 20s, a trip from Guelph to Niagara Falls really was an "all day affair" in a Model "T" Ford. "You left at 7 in the morning, spent 20 minutes at the Falls and arrived back home at 11 at night. During the trip, you usually had to fix a minimum of five flats. Scraped knuckles were always expected!"

R.A.M. Stewart

133 Mr. Brown, in the doorway of his Cork Street bicycle shop around 1920, made enough profit from bicycle sales to buy the car at the left.

R.A.M. Stewart

134

135   Dr. John Howitt stares intently while having his picture taken around 1865. He was "of a singularly self sacrificing nature, giving up almost all of his time and talent to suffering humanity without looking for fee or reward." Dr. Howitt died at the untimely age of 44 in 1870. This much liked man was buried under his favourite tree on the family property.

Guelph's first doctor was not held, it seems, in as high regard. Known as the "mad doctor," he lived in a log house without any doors. Entrance to his home was gained through a square hole 6 feet above the ground. He treated two patients — both died.   R.A.M. Stewart

136   The Guelph General Hospital, 1875. On opening day, August 16, 1875, the first patient admitted was a 73 year old woman who had dysentery — she stayed 28 days.
                                        R.A.M. Stewart

137   By the time this photograph was taken in 1905 the General Hospital had 90 beds. "The Victoria Jubilee Wing" was built in 1887 (right) and the "Alberta Wing" was added in 1897 (left). Blessed B. Sinner, a highly respected man, was the steward for the hospital from 1886 until 1921. His job description:
1. *keep the books*
2. *manage the hospital farm (this farm supplied milk and vegetables till about 1940)*
3. *assist at operations*
4. *instruct the nurses*
5. *dispense the drugs*
6. *collect and distribute the mail*
7. *buy hospital supplies*
8. *look after correspondence.*

The Royal Hotel Collection

138 Guelph's isolation hospital was built in 1911. Although the threat of such dread epidemic diseases as diptheria, smallpox, cholera and typhoid fever may now have ended, older generation Guelphites vividly remember the ravages of these diseases. There were 12 patients with smallpox in the isolation hospital in 1919. Sanitary Inspector H.D. Merewether received a $200 honorarium from a grateful Guelph citizenry for looking after these patients. Wally Beadle

139 St. Joseph's Hospital was established in 1861 by the compassionate Sisters of St. Joseph. This postcard picture of the much altered building was taken about 1905. In 1926, a health survey of 3,558 Guelph children revealed only 1,095 to be in normal health. Today, new medical procedures, drugs and sophisticated electronic instruments have helped make life in Guelph a lot healthier.

Wally Beadle

St. Joseph Hospital, Guelph.

The Manor, Homewood Sanitarium, Guelph, Canada

140 "The Homewood" about 1905. This private psychiatric hospital on Delhi Street was established by a group of Toronto business men in 1883. Guelph was picked because it afforded a quiet, rural, stress-free setting. Wally Beadle

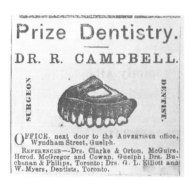

Prize Dentistry.

DR. R. CAMPBELL.

OFFICE, next door to the ADVERTISER office, Wyndham Street, Guelph.
REFERENCES—Drs. Clarke & Orton, McGuire, Herod, McGregor and Cowan, Guelph; Drs. Buchanan & Philips, Toronto; Drs. G. L. Elliott and W. Myers, Dentists, Toronto.

This testimonial to a cure-all remedy appeared in an 1898 letter-to-the-editor:

Dear Sirs: For years I was troubled with periodic sick headaches, being affected usually every Sunday, and was treated by almost every doctor in Guelph with no avail. I was induced by a neighbour to try Sloan's Indian Tonic. A few doses gave immediate relief and one bottle and a half a complete cure. This was three years ago. W.C. Keough

...Many oldtime patent medicines contained such drugs as arsenic, strychnine, cocaine, morphine and alcohol. One potent over-the-counter medicine for "ladies' complaints" had 18% alcohol in it! Beginning in 1908, strict government control started to change all that.

2,820 GUELPH CHILDRENS' TEETH WERE EXAMINED IN 1926 — TOOTH DEFECTS NUMBERED 10,606

141   The dedicated looking Guelph General Hospital graduating nurses' class of 1897.
Wrote Guelph Poet James Gay in 1891:
*Nurses, too—not forgetting you—for us
          you have done your best
And when you are called to leave this
                    wicked world
In Heaven your souls will be at rest.*
Guelph General Hospital

142 A "ghost"* seemingly standing guard at the front steps of the St. George's Church in the square about 1870. The first St. George's Church, built in the square in 1833, was a wooden structure. The church you see in this photograph was constructed in 1851. When it was demolished in 1873, the limestone blocks were used to build a large Queen Street home called "Gilnockie."

*The "ghost" is easily explained. Photography was still in its infancy when this picture was snapped. Nineteenth century film exposure time took up to two minutes; long enough for a person to leave a "shadow" from moving in and out of an operating camera's view. Portraits were torturous in those days. Head-rests, arm supports and other props were used to lock people in position during picture taking sessions.

R.A.M. Stewart

143 Downtown Guelph in 1868. St. George's Church is in the square. To the right, is the original Wellington Hotel built in 1848.

144 *A True Story?*

In the late 1800s, one supposed Guelph corpse looked "too natural" to be dead. There were rumours that the man had been buried alive. The cemetery caretaker's wife said that she had even heard moans from the coffin. Under pressure from the family of the deceased, the police chief ordered the grave to be opened. The chief, accompanied by an undertaker and a doctor, found that the man was, indeed, dead.

145   Guelph citizens long associated the names Mitchell and Tovell with the undertaking business. Guelph's old "Burying Grounds" once occupied the City's Baker Street parking lot — the coffins were moved to Woodlawn Cemetery in 1885. In the lower left corner of this 1873 photograph is the demolition rubble from the former St. George's Church which stood in the square.

R.A.M. Stewart

146 The owners of the carriages are probably inside the post office picking up their mail (1879). This ornate building in St. George's Square was built in 1876. Mail facilities were first set up in a wing of Guelph's first building, "The Priory," July 6, 1828. In the earliest days, mail arrived once a week and letter recipients were notified through lists published in the newspaper.

147 The Post Office has a prominent position in this view of St. George's Square in 1904. A third storey was added to the building in 1902. Louis Watts, a Wyndham Street barber, received the first mail carrier letter on November 7, 1907. The original Bank of Commerce building, built in 1884, is at the far right. The former Royal Bank building is at the far left.

The Royal Hotel Collection

148 The southwest corner of St. George's Square around the turn of the century. R.A.M. Stewart

149 Hearn's Block in 1905. Broadfoot's Red Cross Pharmacy operated in this building for some years... "Careful attention is given to the compounding of physicians' prescriptions and family recipes, none but the freshest and purest drugs and other ingredients being used," declared a 1908 ad. Notice Sam Lee Hing's Chinese Laundry three doors to the left of the drugstore.

Wally Beadle

150 Well-known dentist, Dr. Richard Mahoney had his office in this building for many years. Businesses in the lower floor stores came and went frequently during the building's lifetime. This photograph was taken in the early 1970s, just before the building was removed.

151 The Royal Bank Building, 1976.

152 Joseph Tovell had this building built in 1881. Tovell operated a harness and saddlery shop in the building until the Royal Bank took over in 1906. Mayor John Hamilton is holding the reins of the horses pulling the Guelph Fire Brigade's float in the 1904 Labour Day parade. (Chief Adam Robertson is seated to his right.) The Bank of Montreal provided its Guelph branch manager with a the home to the left.

153   The Tovell Building housed the Royal Bank until 1972. Another long time occupant was Kelso's Printing shop. A Kelso sign can be seen between the 2nd and 3rd storeys in this 1944 photograph.

154 Early in 1974, demolition crews quickly removed the last old stone building in the square. The Guelph Daily Mercury

155 The once proud Tovell building is gone.

156 The new building on the site was opened in the Spring of 1975.

158   Trying to drum up business in downtown Guelph about 1920. Shoppers were enticed to buy in tune with the musical strains of the Guelph Jazz Band musicians as they rode up and down Wyndham Street in a Guelph street car. Notice that the trolley pole was even bent for the occasion.   Wally Beadle

45 QUEBEC STREET

Guelph, Ont._____192

TO **MAHONEY BROS.,** DR.

Sanitary Engineers

Steam and Gas Fitting, Steam and Hot Water Heating, Etc.

RMS CASH   TELEPHONE 20

159   Bill Header for Mahoney Bros.

160   The plumbers of "Mahoney Bros." stand in front of their Quebec Street shop in 1908. Richard Mahoney is in the doorway. Plumber Harry Mahoney (far right) was the Mayor of Guelph in 1915 and 1916. For the convenience of the thirsty passer-by, Mahoney Bros. installed Guelph's first downtown water fountain (left, behind vertical advertising sign) in front of their business premises.   Mrs. V.W. Burrows

161   "The Three R's" in 1905 — Three generations of "Richards." Left to right: Grandfather Richard Mahoney, a Guelph contractor; Grandson Richard Linfield Mahoney (later to become dentist, Dr. R.L. Mahoney); plumber Richard Mahoney jr.   Dr. R.L. Mahoney

162 Does anyone want to stock the shoeshelves? The name "McArthur" was long associated with shoe sales in Guelph. The building is located on the northwest corner of Wyndham and Macdonell streets. Photographer Lionel O'Keeffe took this picture around 1915. (Note his sign, upper left) He humbly advertised that his pictures were "first-class in every particular, in fidelity to original or copy, graceful and natural in pose, and unsurpassed in design, execution and finish." Other well-known nineteenth and early-twentieth century Guelph photographers were: D.H. Booth; C.H. Burgess; R.B. Kennedy; and, W. Marshall. Originally, they took most of the pictures in this book.

The Royal Hotel Collection

164 Finlay & Molloy operated a St. George's Square barber shop in the days before men's hairstyling. (February 24, 1920) L. to R.: Mr. Molloy, Mr. Finlay, customer (Is he bald?), **Mr. Warden.**

DOWNTOWN

An 1887 Guelph By-law:
"Within the limits of this municipality no night soil or contents of any cesspool be removed unless previously deodorized and during its transportation the material shall be covered with a layer of fresh earth, except the removal shall have been by some 'odourless excavating process'."

163 "For 36 years he has been at work beautifying Guelph with his brush"... 1908 ad. The employees of "Barber the Painter" pose in front of the St. George's Square shop around 1905.

The Royal Hotel Collection

165 Laying Guelph's first sewer pipes in St. George's Square in 1903.

Society

166 Wearing the latest Guelph styles about 1890.. (L. to R.) Laura, Arthur and Alice Higinbotham.

R.A.M. Stewart

"In the great Department Stores and Fashion Shops, Colonial Company Created Dresses — made in Guelph — are favoured by shrewd merchandisers and customers, and are accepted as Fashion's leading interpretations of prevailing modes." (1927 Ad)

167 Did Guelphite Arthur Cutten (centre, black suit) just tell a joke? If he did, it looks as if Connie Cutten (standing to right of Arthur) has heard it before.

R.A.M. Stewart

168 The inside of grocer W.H. Fielding's store in 1906. A part of his 1906 advertisement emphasized: "Mr. Fielding has never resorted to anything that was sensational in order to gain trade ... he holds his customers by giving them good prices, good service and good delivery."
Elizabeth Gray

169 Harry and Edith Mahoney with their dog. Look at those spires on Edith's hat! (c.1900)
Dr. R.L. Mahoney

170 Guelph teenage girls, 1917. Talking about boys?

171 A Guelph family gathering, Dominion Day, 1923. Oh, what can be read in a face!

172 The "Kandy Kitchen", a favourite gathering spot on lower Wyndham Street. "In the old days, it was a big thing on a Saturday to go to the show and then to the Kandy Kitchen for a big dish of ice cream." Charles Yeates, of Royal Dairy fame, established this ice cream parlour in 1899. (Photograph date: 1905.) Mrs. V.W. Burrows

173 A 1970's descendant of the Kandy Kitchen.

174 Proprietor Lloyd Taylor (right) and his assistant George Jones stand in the doorway (1930) of Taylor's well known grocery store on the northwest corner of Eramosa Road and Arthur Street. In 1928, a local grocer was featuring canned tomatoes at 6 cans for 77¢. Aileen Cooke

Opera House, Guelph.

175   The grand opening for the Griffin Royal Opera House occurred on the night of November 5, 1894.
The O'Keefe & Wales Opera Company staged the
comic opera "Athenia." Many well-known Canadian
and United States performers (including Guelph's
own world famous star, Edward Johnson) played the
Opera House. In 1953 it was ripped down and replaced with the building presently occupied by
Simpson-Sears and the Odeon Theatre.

Wally Beadle

176   Throughout his career, Johnson played many
important operatic roles. The spirit of this simple,
yet unexplainedly complex man, lives on through
the Edward Johnson Music Foundation. The Foundation, since 1968, has sponsored the annual Guelph
Spring Festival. By featuring a wide range of talen-
ted artists from various musical, theatrical and lit-
erary fields, the highly acclaimed Spring Festival
is achieving its single, clear objective: Everyone can
enjoy the arts!   R.A.M. Stewart

177   Guelph's musical giant, Edward Johnson.
"Eddie," as he was known to everyone in Guelph,
carefully saved up $100 to pay for a trip to New York
for an audition. Little did anyone realize that this
shy, reserved, former St. George's Church choir
tenor soloist would rise to the top of the operatic
music world.   R.A.M. Stewart

EDWARD JOHNSON

THE 'CARUSO' OF CANADA

3-8

IT'S 1901, AND A STARRY-EYED **SINGER** FROM GUELPH, ONTARIO, FINDS HIMSELF IN NEW YORK TO STUDY MUSIC.

WALT McDAYTER NORMAN DREW

THAT YOUTH, EDWARD JOHNSON, SEES HIS FIRST OPERA THERE, AND MAKES A SOLEMN PROMISE...

ONE DAY IT'LL BE **ME** SINGING ON THAT STAGE!

IT'S A VERY NERVOUS JOHNSON WHO, AFTER YEARS OF STUDY, AUDITIONS FOR A NEW OPERETTA, "THE WALTZ DREAM".

AUDITIONS TODAY

IF I HAVE ANY TALENT AT ALL... I MUST PROVE IT **NOW**!

LUCKY BREAK FOR THE YOUNG CANADIAN! JOHNSON GETS THE LEAD TENOR ROLE IN "THE WALTZ DREAM" AND THRILLS AT HIS NAME IN LIGHTS ON **BROADWAY**.

WITH EDWARD JOHNSON

3-9

BUT NOT AS THRILLED AS WHEN A FRIEND SURPRISES HIM WITH...

EDDIE, I'VE ASKED **ENRICO CARUSO** TO LISTEN TO YOU SING...AND HE'S AGREED!

JOHNSON SINGS FOR CARUSO, AND HE'S TOLD...

YOU'LL ONE DAY BE A GREAT TENOR! GO TO FLORENCE, MY BOY, STUDY WITH MY OLD TEACHER, VINCENZO LOMBARDI!

WALT McDAYTER NORMAN DREW

JOHNSON FOLLOWS CARUSO'S ADVICE AND STUDIES IN ITALY. BY 1912 HE'S READY FOR HIS DEBUT AT PADUA, UNDER THE STAGE NAME OF **EDUARDO DI GIOVANNI**.

EDUARDO DI GIOVANNI

3-10

THOUGH BIASED AGAINST NORTH AMERICAN SINGERS, THE ITALIANS LOVE THE TENOR FROM GUELPH. HE WINS THEIR PRAISE IN ROME WITH "THE GIRL OF THE GOLDEN WEST"...

BRAVO!

HE'S ANOTHER CARUSO!

...THEN HE SIGNS UP WITH **LA SCALA** OPERA HOUSE, MILAN, AND WINS THE ACCLAIM OF THE CONTINENT FOR HIS LEAD IN WAGNER'S "PARSIFAL"

WALT McDAYTER NORMAN DREW

WORLD WAR I ENDS. EDWARD JOHNSON SINGS WITH LA SCALA UNTIL 1920, WHEN...

I'VE ACCEPTED AN OFFER FROM THE CHICAGO OPERA COMPANY.

NOT ALL HIS PERFORMANCES ARE SUCCESSES. AT ONE OUTDOOR OPERA IN CHICAGO, HE OPENS HIS MOUTH TO SING--AND **SWALLOWS** A BUTTERFLY!

3-12

HE GOES ON TOUR, AND BECOMES THE FIRST CANADIAN OPERA SINGER TO EVER BE APPLAUDED IN THE ORIENT.

BUT HIS GREATEST HONOR COMES IN 1922. HE'S SIGNED UP WITH NEW YORK'S **METROPOLITAN** OPERA COMPANY-- MECCA OF THE OPERA WORLD!

WALT McDAYTER NORMAN DREW

IN 1935 JOHNSON'S PROMOTED FROM SINGER TO **GENERAL MANAGER** OF THE METROPOLITAN OPERA! HE REVOLUTIONIZES OPERA BY MAKING IT AVAILABLE TO ALL NORTH AMERICANS THROUGH RADIO.

ON THE AIR

WALT McDAYTER NORMAN DREW

BUT HE MISSES CANADA, AND IN 1950 RETURNS TO BECOME CHAIRMAN OF TORONTO'S **ROYAL CONSERVATORY OF MUSIC**.

3-13

THE FINAL CURTAIN FALLS ON EDWARD JOHNSON IN 1959. HE DIES IN GUELPH...BUT HIS NAME LIVES ON AS AN INSPIRATION TO ALL YOUNG CANADIANS WHO LONG TO FIND FAME ON THE OPERA STAGES OF THE WORLD!

BOOKS TO READ:

'CANADIAN PORTRAITS', LOUISE McCREADY, CLARKE IRWIN ;

'ENCYCLOPEDIA CANADIANA', VOLUME 5, GROLIER SOCIETY.

180 Everyone loves a parade! A surging crowd of Guelph citizens line the 1912 Dominion Day Parade route. Look at all the bunting on the buildings!

Wally Beadle

181 The Bricklayers and Masons float in a turn of the century Labour Day parade. The D.E. MacDonald Brothers building (right) is on the southwest corner of Wyndham and Macdonell streets.

R.A.M. Stewart

182 Lower Wyndham Street in 1908. A Labour Day parade is in progress. Notice the sign that says: "Labor Omnia Vincit."

Wally Beadle

EVERYONE LOVES A PARADE

183 A horse drawn carriage and marching band pass through St. George's Square during the 1908 Old Home Week parade. The sign over the blacksmith fountain reads: "There is No Place Like Home." After annual Old Home Week parades, there would be such crowd thrillers as a "Dare-Devil Dash by Prof. Zavaro" or a "Balloon Ascension and Parachute Drop by Prof. Tardini."

R.A.M. Stewart

184 Here comes the circus! A circus parade passes Trafalgar Square (Woolwich St. at Eramosa Rd.) on its way to Johnson's field. (c.1920)

R.A.M. Stewart

185 The Sparks Circus visited Guelph June 29, 1927. The elephants carried advertisements for the Chevrolet car sold by Daymond Motors.

Dr. R.L. Mahoney

186 It's hard to believe, but Guelph's huge Canadian Centennial Day parade happened 10 years ago!

E.A. Coulman

187 The Guelph Musical Society Band about 1905. Organized in 1898, this band is now known as the "Guelph Concert Band."

Chris V. Robinson

188 The "Robinson Bakery Band" could be hired to play at any function: Lawn Socials, Garden Parties; Concerts; and, Fairs. Also in their ad: "with comedians if required." Besides the bakery band, there was a smaller nine-member family band which is seen in this 1925 photograph. Front Row—L. to R.: Mr. Robinson, Robert, Ted jr., Ted sr. Back Row: Albert, George, Ernest, Arthur, Chris.

Chris V. Robinson

189 Guelph had its own John Denver in the 1920s. He was a member of the "Guelph Jazz Band"... This photograph of the band was snapped in the early twenties during "Shop in Guelph Week."

Kneeling L. to R.: Bob O'Connor, Tom Cavanagh, Hilt Jeans jr.
Standing, middle row:
    Hilt Jeans sr., Ernie Wilson, Enoch Hazelwood, Chris Robinson.
Back row:
    Charlie Beadle (motorman for special "Shop in Guelph" streetcar), a mystery person, John Denver!, Alf Cavanagh.

Wally Beadle

190 Outdoor band concerts were very popular in Guelph until a few years ago. This is the Exhibition Park bandstand around 1910.

Mrs. D.C. Savage

FIRST DAY OF ISSUE   JOUR D'EMISSION

IN MEMORIAM

1872 † 1918

"In Flanders fields the poppies blow"

Lieutenant Colonel

JOHN McCRAE

Canadian Army Medical Corps

Soldier-Physician-Poet

Famous Canadians Series

ROSE CRAFT

193   A group of mounted soldiers ride up Wyndham Street in May, 1916.

194   Looking almost like tin soldiers, the members of Guelph's 1st Volunteer Rifle Co. stand stiffly at attention after having been inspected by the Adjutant General of the Militia, Baron de Rottenberg. The date of this momentous occasion was Thursday, October 15, 1857. In stark contrast to this military display is St. Bartholomew's Church looming ominously in the background.

During the American Civil War, a Guelph firm, Robertson's Foundry, manufactured cannons, cannonballs and hand-grenades for the Confederate army. The arms were shipped in boxes marked "potatoes."

R.A.M. Stewart

In Flanders Fields

In Flanders fields the poppies blow
Between the crosses, row on row,
That mark our place; and in the sky
The larks, still bravely singing, fly
Scarce heard amid the guns below.

We are the Dead. Short days ago
We lived, felt dawn, saw sunset glow,
Loved, and were loved, and now we lie
    In Flanders Fields.

Take up our quarrel with the foe:
To you from failing hands we throw
The torch; be yours to hold it high.
If ye break faith with us who die
We shall not sleep, though poppies grow
    In Flanders fields

John McCrae

Colonel John McCrae Memorial
Branch No. 257

195   Guelph's Carnegie library was completed in 1905. American steel magnate, Andrew Carnegie, paid the $24,000 bill. (Photograph date: c.1910)

The Public Archives of Canada

WHICH SIDE
WOULD YOU HAVE BEEN ON?

Some Guelph residents have been irritated by its hodge podge of architectural styles ranging from baroque to the classic. It has been described as a building of terrifying proportions and elephantine decorations. But other Guelph residents think the structure is a beautiful and outstanding building that lends a touch of exotic glamour to their city.
        . . .The Guelph Daily Mercury, 1964

196   The wrecking crew dealt the old library's dome a final blow at 1:24 pm, Monday, December 7, 1964.   The Guelph Daily Mercury

JIMMY GAY

POET OF THE DAY

197   Self-styled "Poet Laureate of Canada," Guelph's own James Gay, "The Poet of the Day." He ranked himself with Tennyson and Longfellow. . .
(Photograph date: c. 1880)
R.A.M. Stewart

I came on earth a natural born poet,
And for the good of my fellow-men
    the world will soon know it;
My talents received are too bright understand,
Even to be buried in the sand.

198   An aerial view of downtown Guelph in September, 1947. Starting at St. George's Square, trace each one of the streets radiating out from the square ...Quite a few changes have occurred in just 30 years!

George Cooke

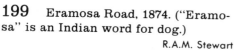

201

199 Eramosa Road, 1874. ("Eramosa" is an Indian word for dog.)

R.A.M. Stewart

200 Eramosa Road about 1887. Note the Trafalgar Park bandstand to the left. Look carefully at the homes in the background of this photograph. Many of these homes are still standing.

R.A.M. Stewart

202 During removal operations, June 2, 1964, a workman prematurely cut a supporting crossmember. The whole structure then collapsed. The house to the right (now removed) was the second home to be built on that side of the river.

HOW ERAMOSA ROAD HAS CHANGED IN 100 YEARS

203 "Riverslea," once owned by nineteenth century miller, James Goldie, is now a part of the Homewood. For $13 a month in 1885, you could rent the new 8 room brick house at 32 Cambridge Street. It had a bathroom and city water, hard and soft. The 6 room brick house next door was a little cheaper to rent: $8 a month.

The Royal Hotel Collection

204 "Wyoming," built in 1866-67, was owned for many years by J.W. Lyon, originator of the World Publishing Company. Reputed to be Guelph's first millionaire, Lyon gave a hint as to what helped him amass his fortune — in a glowingly descriptive 1928 sales booklet for his Queen Street home, he stated frugally: "Guelph is desirable for many reasons. One is it is a very cheap place to live."

The Royal Hotel Collection

205 Overlooking Exhibition Park is "Parkview," a majestically turreted home built around 1894 by downtown department store owner G.B. Ryan. A good deal? In 1881, T.J. Day bought John Horsman's huge home "Prospect Place" and four acres of land on Grange Street for $6,500. Horsman had paid over $18,000 a few years earlier.

The Royal Hotel Collection

207 This group of homes on Queen Street, seen here about 1910, was dubbed by many as "Millionaires Row."

Wally Beadle

206

208 St. George's Square from the city hall tower in 1874. St. George's Church had been removed a year earlier.

R.A.M. Stewart

Post Office and Wyndham Street, looking North, Guelph, Ont.

209 The Square, 1905. Notice the sanitation department's bucket wagon (centre) for the removal of good old-fashioned horsebuns! The word "Gasoline" is on the side of the tank wagon (right).

Wally Beadle

THE SQUARE

210 In all its resplendent glory! The 1915 St. George's Square. *Wally Beadle*

211 St. George's Square, 1942. *Wally Beadle*

212 The 1954 version of St. George's Square. *Wally Beadle*

213 "A Royal Welcome to the Royal City"...Old Home Week, 1908.

The Royal Hotel Collection

All things are laid out beautiful, as you take your walks around,
You can travel again for thousands of miles,
None such again are found.
You travel east, you travel west, return to Guelph, say it's best.

....James Gay, 1875

A WORD ABOUT THIS BOOK . . . (and some advice, too)

Six years ago, I was asked by Ron Eyre (Educational Media Centre, Wellington County Board of Education) if I would take about 300 teachers on a field trip. "Yes," was the answer — the figure "300" presented the organizational challenge I liked.

"Where can we go on our field trip?" I thought. The answer came quickly. I had just finished taking a series of excellent University of Guelph lectures presented largely in an old school bus which bounced, bumped and careened its way around Guelph and area. My decision: use downtown Guelph as an outdoor classroom.

"Guelphscape 70", a 49 page walking tour guide was the result. The downtown Guelph field trip was no mean trick for an ex-Torontonian — I had to learn a great deal about Guelph's history in a terrible hurry. I'm still at it.

"Guelphscape 70" set the stage for this book.

Where did I get the old photographs and information?

First the photographs . . .

Many came from those dusty, old albums you find in the attic. If you look back at the picture credits, you might recognize the name of a friend or two. Many interesting hours were spent reminiscing with these people about the subjects or objects in their album photos. Next time you look at an old family photo, look carefully over the shoulder of dear, departed "Aunty" — in the background, there might be an old building, car, or train of interest to the amateur (or professional) historian.

Modern photographic equipment will allow the clear reproduction of even the smallest detail in an old photo.

Advice: take the time to jot down the names of the people in your photographs. (Some details about the event would be nice, too.) A must: record the date! Your photos might appear in a similar book 100 years from now! The lack of dates and names has to be the most frustrating thing a photograph collector faces.

Mr. Robert Stewart's picture collection deserves a special mention. For many years, he has been avidly scouring Guelph for old photos — his collection must number at least 20,000 photos!

Many of the photographs were obtained from old postcards. Virtually all of the postcards I used came from Wally Beadle's large collection. Wally explains the importance of the postcard like this: "Now look, the postcard has been providing a photographic history of places since around the turn of the century. They had few telephones in those days so they sent postcards instead. Some of the messages were pretty cute — you get a look into the private lives of people — how they lived — what they worried about. The postoffice even dated the picture for you!"

Wally's advice: "Keep buying current postcards, in ten years they'll be valuable."

Other photographs were loaned to me by the Guelph Police Department and Ted Ernst, who is the Guelph Fire Department's special historian.

The information . . .

A good deal of the historical information came from the books available in the "Guelph Section" of the Guelph Public Library. As well, I used a number of publications produced by the Guelph Historical Society.

Other sources were old catalogues and industrial brochures, once again, found in numerous Guelph attics.

One major source of information was The Guelph Mercury's 1927 Centennial issue. This was a truly remarkable issue — it had 132 pages and was just crammed with historical information. A photocopy is available at the library — I was lucky enough to borrow a cherished copy from a friend of mine, Marie Ridd.

A Mercury carrier of the day well remembers the issue: "It was awful heavy. Oh, how I cursed — under my breath, of course — each one two inches thick, mind you!" She added: "I wish I'd kept a few, but those were the days when you heaved everything out after you'd finished." (There are probably no more than 6 to 8 copies of this issue remaining in Guelph.)

It's amazing how the news accounts of today become the history of tomorrow. I had complete access to The Guelph Daily Mercury files and photographs. The Mercury staff members were very generous to me. I'll never forget the day (5 p.m. — the paper was on the street) when I was searching for some obscure fact with three newspaper helpers — a former city editor and two reporters. On that occasion, only the city editor was helpful (He found the fact, too!), the two reporters bogged down looking at an "old" 1960 Corvair ad . . . "Gee, that looks funny!" said one of them. That's what nostalgia does!

Ring, Ring, Ring (quiet, reserved voice at the other end as I press the phone to my ear) "Hullo Don, this is Mike McDonald of Ampersand calling — John Denison over at Boston Mills Press wants to know how the book's coming along." Answer: "Well, I'm workin' on it — didn't know a book was so much work!" (I told him that exactly 102 times.) The thoughts and ideas Mike and John presented to me added much to this book!

Looking back, was it worth it? "Yes . . . I think."

Happy Birthday, Guelph!

Donald E. Coulman